Running at Hendry's

The Sum (1958, Alan Swallow)

Between Matter and Principle (1963, Alan Swallow)

The Heat Lightning (1967, Bowdoin College Museum of Art)

Tree Meditation and Others (1970, Swallow Press)

White River Poems (1976, Swallow Press)

In Plain Air (1982, Swallow Press)

Water Among the Stones (1987, privately printed)

Stubble Burning (1988, Robert L. Barth)

Goodbye Matilija (1992, Living Batch Press)

The White Boat (1995, Buckner Press)

Away from the Road (1998, Living Batch Press)

Collected Poems (2012, Dowitcher Press)

Selected Poems (2012, Dowitcher Press)

Running at Hendry's: Sonnets (2012, Dowitcher Press)

Alan Stephens

RUNNING AT HENDRY'S

Edited by A.A. Stephens

Dowitcher Press
Santa Barbara, California

Contents

Author's Note

I've always loved the old sonnet sequences more than any of the sonnets in them, magnificent or lovely as these may be. The sequences take up as no single poem can the unpredictable mix of experiences and themes with the prevailing passion, all going on during a longish stretch of time. Then there are the scraps of narrative that come out incidentally, the shifts (alas) in the passion itself, the sense that each poem is being done at a sitting with the time passing, that an idea that doesn't come through satisfactorily here may turn up later (only now with a fresh secondary theme jostling it which later becomes itself a main theme), the untidy couplings of metaphysics and peevishness, jealousy or other unworthy emotions, this or that unrelated preoccupation obtruding along the way, the speaker himself changing willy-nilly, the bits of news, glooms, dull stretches, elations—and the old types, the anniversary sonnet, the insomniac sonnet, the sonnet about the sonnet.

When I found myself taking up running at the height of the craze, a byproduct was that phrases kept coming to mind, pieces of poems, having to do not only with running but also with the not especially beautiful or otherwise remarkable beach where I ran. I had come to love the place for its shapes, tones, smells and the rest, not least the people that showed up there. All this, with its daily, hourly changeableness, I was each day looking forward obsessively to visiting. So here was a passion, and it occurred to me that I could cross the new craze with an old craze and do a sonnet sequence, drawing on whatever came in handy in the older craze, for treatment of what I was doing down at Hendry's nearly every day, over the weeks, the months, the unspectacular seasons.

A.S.

Running at Hendry's

After Work: Foreword

Home, then out of the canyon and inch past
Shopping center, school; inch over freeway;
Veer with the creek that notches the pale clay
Headlands and I am at the place at last.
The shoreline hereabouts runs east and west.
Clear days there's islands to be seen, any day
Sky, sand, waves, light, birds, dogs, people. I'd say
Late in the day in winter is when it's best.
Down the long, slant beach, and the wave-tips catch
The sun's low fire, the wet sand's all red light,
The shorebirds eat red light—and all goes gray
The moment you turn back the other way,
Cliffs, sea, and sky a great cave, in dead light;
And the fresh darkness settling, in the stretch.

Down Here After Being Kept Away
Three Weeks by Sickness

How much I missed this place. While I've been gone
The season has turned, the winter birds are here,
The sand is firm, clean, smooth, and the air clear
With a wave flashing cold in the low sun
Under the slow wingbeats of a pelican
That three pilfering gulls keep swinging near,
Whimbrels and godwits and plovers and killdeer
Work the sleek shallows, I begin to run:
Easy, now. But I swear the beach gives back
My footthuds like the tightly stretched buckskin
It looks like here, the blazing water track
Of the sun's running beside me—coming in
The old ocean commotion and the dark mass
Of a jogging girl's hair jouncing as we pass.

Commotion

Under a low fogbank, the blackish tone
Of its belly darkening the waves and sand
And cliffs that block all view of the high land
Where the town sits in sunlight, I'm alone,
The beach is bare, the hard brown sand slopes down
Steeply to the low tide. From where I stand
No jogger rounds the point to scare the band
Of godwits from their meal. I'll start my run
Together with the dark sea running in
From a horizon turning steely bright
(Sun finishing its run where the fog's thin)
While jaegers and gulls keep up a running fight
Whirling sharp black against that piece of sky
The beach and cliffs run toward and likewise I.

3

Liberté, Fraternité

More fog.—Have you seen a gross, heavy-legged deer?
Or in a flight of terns some with the bill
Twisted and blunt, some with stub wings, some small
As wrens? Imagine an ectomorphic bear.
No, shaped by the shapes of water and earth and air
They move in ruthless grace and crucial skill
Unfree and strong and evenly beautiful,
Unprovided with souls, completely clear and here.
I pass a poor old woman, six foot three,
Mannish, who has a heron's jerky stride,
Just as a well-built fellow passes me.
Next, hairy breasts swinging from side to side,
An obese youth rounds the point; and better weather
Brings many another of us out here together.

4

Beach Litter

Slipped through the fingers of my writing-hand
Already in these dozen days or so—
The grove of winter trees, intaglio
Complete with twigs, carved in the hard smooth sand
(While the waves keep rushing in to land
In the old uproar) by the trickling backflow,
And running in fog, and the young pair who go
Down beach apart, I see the fellow stand
With his back to her while she with her eyes
Downward walks this way, that way—coming in
I pass and hear her humming cheerfully,
And the cold light one dusk far out at sea
And the time I finished fast as if to win,
Some girl's clear laugh away down the beach the prize:

—Or the man and the old woman seated at either end
Of a long bench that leans and sags rustily:
Though sudden raw weather has cleared the beach, and she
Is dressed none too warmly, she keeps with a thin hand
Her jacket collar closed and reads on as she'd planned,
It looks like, in an old paperback, all the while he
Dressed up as for a party—a party refugee?—
Stares, with his elbows on his knees, at the cold sand:
Or the leopard seal lying long dead and swollen tight
Getting his spots changed for him, all right, by the sea
And the sea air: or that strong old man in serious thought,
Bareheaded, in a workman's clothes—a machinist, maybe;
The last runner in, I met him stalking doggedly out
Between dark sea and cliffs in the fast-failing light.

6

The Pelican-watcher (1)

Dusk under fog; and under fog a mist
Grays out the view three hundred yards off shore;
Ocean, though wind's no harder than before,
Smashes and roars where it had slapped and hissed
All week long; beach may be at its ugliest
Heaped up with kelp torn from the ocean floor,
Huge clots and strings of it, yellowy brown, and more
Comes heaving and sprawling in on every crest.
Few birds. It's townsfolk out for the spectacle
And hundreds of surfers: black torsos holding still
As tree stumps in the troughs, awaiting the right one.
No pelicans. I miss them, on my run.
Then, five of them! infixing their reflection
In the wave's wall they fly along to perfection.

7

The Pelican-watcher (2)

15

There must have been five hundred here last week
Not grazing the waves like these but swirling high
Their silhouettes jagged against a sky
Bright silver in the west over a sleek
And blazing evening sea; slow, homely, meek
Amongst the agile lovely terns and sly
Gull gangs they flapped deliberately by.
Ungainly dives get them the fish they seek.
They look like so much scrap-iron hurled in the air,
But they belong. Archaic and venerable
Their ugliness no less than their steady skill
(And now alas who's jogging toward me there?
A handsome colleague whose talk is a display
Of intellectual cowardice and decay…).

Running with My Sons

Two of them home by chance the same weekend!
I fight a fear that's like Ben Jonson's fear,
Of being too glad of having them down here
Running abreast with me on the hard smooth sand.
And all the better it is for being unplanned:
I have no heed for shorebirds, or the clear
Sunlight inside the wavelets rippling near,
Or other runners, or the familiar blend
Of surf- and gull-noise.—One of them sprints away
Spattering through the shallows like a pup,
I say to the other "Don't let me hold you up,"
And off he spurts. I watch them happily.
How they shine! across the difference of years,
And will shine in my day fears and night fears.

9

Running with My Sons

Fifty-one runs with nineteen and twenty-three
Thinking "by hap of happy hap," the phrase
Cast by the crude old Tudor well displays
The kinship of happiness and luck … I see
From the corner of my eye how springily
The boys are striding, how their breathing stays
Easy and light. Not so with them always,
Both once rode crutches after surgery.
We round the second point and they run on
Into the haze, down beach I've never run,
While I turn back, and think of how that stretch
They're running is like the years I'll never reach;
And think helplessly, how will it be for them?
It'll be the same and sharply not the same.

More Hap

Bad omen in the morning and once more
Late in the day, encountering face to face
Two sons of bitches, each at a time and place
I'd never seen either one of them before.
And the day, picketed by this polluting pair,
Went wrong; running in the dusk I now retrace
The slight brain-lurches that put me off my pace …
The slippages of heed that are my despair!
So I run along full of my latest blunder—
And everything's still, but a distant simmering
From the sea, the light rakes low, the tide is neap,
In the strange peace I nearly halt in wonder
At water in thin clear layers wavering
On the flat sand—a kind of shining sleep.

Delights of Winter Evenings Down Here

Saturday night. The ranger's shut the gate.
In the deep dusk I make his figure out
Eyeing me as I wheel the Z about
Five yards from his white gate-bars and hesitate
At the open Exit. Never before so late,
I park on up the road. He has the clout
To turn me back, I half expect his shout
As I slip through the nearly dark parking lot:
Cold wind. Dark sea with sharp little peaks all over.
This long bright strip I'm running on is lighter
Than the sky! Back where the beach is dark some water
Or foam—no, the white patch on a wing is flashing.
Five terns—still seeing fish!—plunge, wheel, hover.
Black stubs of surfers lift on a swell—*that's* passion.

God-light

25

Low dark cloud-cover and ocean make a pair
Of jaws held just apart; in the opening,
Where I now run, no room for anything
But the cliffs, now bleakly pale where they are bare.
At the horizon, a low, cold light just where
The sun has set; I watch it briefly cling
At the sea's rim—clear God-light, the real thing—
While I run on through suddenly darkening air.
Under the cliffs are sanderlings and plovers
Busy with their last feeding for the day;
And a few people—a lone girl there, two lovers,
An old lady with her dog; and part way
Down the cliff ahead a house hangs, with a flight
Of stairs down to the beach, and window light.

13

House

Though days may pass and you'll see no one there
The place is lived in always. There was the sight
You could have seen in clear, still evening light,
Of a girl trimming a bearded young man's hair
Out on the littered deck, and you might hear
The little dog's wow-*wow!* when running late
And alone below; for months a drying skate
Swung under the deck, wetsuits and suchlike gear
Hang from the railings. Looks like a fine life.
Sometimes one of them waves as they come and go
Casually in view of us passersby below,
While they hang half in the air on the steep clay;
That the house is going, waves chewing away,
Is habit-knowledge with them, as between man and wife.

A big storm struck shortly after this was written, some of the cliff gave way, and one of the family was interviewed in the paper: "I know what it's like to live with the sound of concrete popping, but when you love to live here …."

14

Running Late

Last class goes overtime, there's some delay
Getting an ace bandage on an aching knee
At the right tension, and then hurriedly
Into slow, slow traffic: the last light of day
Fades off the clouds above my getaway,
Though there at last and running I can see
The sickle moon reflected, glittery,
Like a surf-perch, in a wave; under the play
Of water sliding in and sliding back,
This sand is a seal's flank, the inch-high hiss
Of that foam edging somehow throws a black
Shadow in this faint light; my emphasis
Was haste-blurred on those lines of Herbert's. How
I'd like to have the class back (briefly!) now.

Running Late, Having Held the Class on Herbert Overtime to Look at Three Lines

Deep dusk, the quarter moon strong enough now
To show in the wave's flank with a fish-like glitter,
I run on the dark beach thinking, This is better
Than the delicate orange clouds two days ago
In pale green sky, too pretty. (Are there no
Other runners here, for once?) Thinking, That wetter
Sand there shines like some membrane, this twitter
Of sleepy sanderlings says it must be so
That I'm the last one out, that subdued roar
Of water's a not-word I have heard before,
And suddenly there comes the one thing more
I ought to have told the class, that not elsewhere
In English is that thought thought—and see how clear
And passionate and quiet it is there.

16

Running Against a Cold Wind

A bleakness about the place, with the wind keen,
Dark ocean under it running like a full
Rough icy river. A bright diagonal
Of orange cloud slopes over the whole scene,
The sky below it's turning that strange pale green
Coleridge in his dejection couldn't feel
The beauty of. I think of the tall girl
Who glanced my way as I came driving in,
And again later as I began my run
And passed her with her friends, and how her presence
Filled for a time the whole place like a fragrance.
Hard going now! lungs hurting, and she long gone
And everyone else but me, the whole scene stark,
Even the cliff house windows staying dark.

And the Fat One Gripping a Bottle of Wine

Blazing November. The wrongness of this weather's what
Makes my being here for anything all wrong, the sea
Having gone slack and pale and bland and summery,
The air since the first light this morning dry and hot
And motionless. Broad day's brought everybody out.
There goes a runner threading through a family
Straggling along in street-clothes. Surfers unseeingly
Step around three elderly ladies. All tramp my holy spot.
I run on sand where multitudes lay and strolled and sat.
It's scuffed and stale. And heading through the overused scene,
Around the last point I see alone out on the flat,
Where the sand's newly wet, one fat girl and one lean
Briefly link arms and dance, whirling this way and that
Over their clear, prancing reflections in the sheen.

Running with a Poem from the
Latest *TLS* in my Head

A hot breath off the land at my turnback spot.
A streak of skunk-scent a little further down.
Sea quiet in the late dusk. No moon
As yet. The hard sand uneven underfoot,
Much trampled on. An airliner's headlight
Makes a big white star in the orange coming on
In thin clouds fanning out from the set sun—
Orange, and a real green, staying clear and bright!
But what I think of's the Britisher with the dripping nose
Who thinks we'll think he's tough because he says
Evil is tough and sure of itself and Good
Is gentle, irresolute. You know how it goes?
St. Thomas More, for instance, living in a daze?
Samuel Johnson, so lacking in hardihood?

19

Moon Measuring

Moon'll be rising. There's a few people here
In the chill of the sundown, some of them regulars—
Old tilt-hat's there on his bench, photographers
Stand waiting for the colors to appear
As the sun drops. Pelicans swing in near
The flat beach where the sea now mildly stirs.
They fly in line, casting a row of blurs
Of pelicans on the slick swells they barely clear....
The boys are home, all three of them this time.
But they ran earlier. Turning back I pause
To watch the dead white half moon on its climb,
Which one of them said, a lunar month ago,
"Looks like a helmet" as he rejoined his slow
Parent along this stretch. And so it does.

20

Sonnet in Printer's Greek

41

Than sky or water. freenn tthom her hands,
How can they see? Bylypsoorr else a lover....
Mallards float in the color. Llcck stobs hover.
Msidli advationfir ent shining bands.
A liitle bleak. yllongg undulant ands.
Smell off slifftop, excloomong. Woll uncover
Not much rmmm. And veers abruptly out over
Face tense. Breathing iv arq demands.
Or flash of foam. Blicypp, old sonneteer …
Abwarss in hero telic imperfection
Whyever not, Considerink the clear
Though sanderlings ssyvrrr which one's direction
Swer.kho in concert almost disappear.
Abdi nec dog runs on the red reflection.

Death Song

43

Not the dead seal swollen tight as a football
That I saw, clear in the midday winter light,
But my students at their final exams last night
Was my death vision. And no, not Nancy's skull
Under her smooth skin. I saw death edge them all
As they toiled there, it rested at the white
Surface of the papers I had, curved with the tight
Curve of the c in 'precise,' kept the interval
Between each letter (and gives this cold salt air
Its underlightness, the moon its bright rim because
Death is what does not happen, around what does),
I held in my lungs its imperishable elsewhere,
I saw creation being supported by
Death's tortoise—not on his shell, in his air-clear eye.

Visitation

No running is the doctor's order. Glumly enough
To walk along and watch the other runners run,
And the sky fires up smoky crimson, and the sun
Slips into a sea suddenly darkening and rough
Out from the shore. Tide's out. Where the sand levels off
And where I like to go, the water's coming on
In terraces, shining layers, the nearest one
So thin it is a skin of light to trudge and scuff
And watch the slowly deepening color on, until
There is my holy of holies: a sandy-floored recess
Under the cliffs, half hidden behind a rock outcrop.
Always when I am running this is where I stop
And turn back. What now? Careful! A brief pause, I guess,
With the merest sidelong glance will do or nothing will.

It was a Greek mistake to connect the sacred with the permanent, the sacred be-
ing phenomenal like everything else, and the transient conjunction of chance and
those necessities whose most apt expression is mathematical. Three weeks after
this poem was done, the holy place was destroyed by the combination of a high
winter tide and huge waves that changed the shapes of the cliff-bases and heaped
storm-wreckage—much of it freshly splintered trees—high up against them.

23

Colleague with a Notebook

Beach wide and flat. I run, dully, on a sheet
Of neutral-colored light, slipping along
In the wet is a blurry quarter moon, a tongue
Of water pushes in quietly over the wet,
Quick-sliding, low-hissing, its tip of foamy white
Entering up the sand. Then I'm among
The seal brown, seal high rocks—old seals and young
Seaward they slant, alertly—exposed of late
By the winter tides ... slowly, on the way back,
Darkness coming, the horizon turns a bright,
Deep orange-red, the exact color of the throat
Of a cutthroat trout! Pass a man writing a note
(His camera's set up) and look back—beach black
Where he stands, crossed with great slashes of light.

24

Loiterer

But the water—a half inch deep there, sidling in,
Rumpling to sharp little ridges, with elegant
Black shadows, in the level light … ripplings sent
At an angle through other ripplings cross-hatch, then
The surface quiets, and, smooth once again,
Shivers all over … two tiny waves, blent
Head-on emerge, each going the way it went …
New water foams in, slides back clear and thin:
The lovely loiterings, with darkness coming on,
Stay with me as I finish up my run,
Having had to hurry all I did today.
And nothing done well, getting it all done.
"That most exciting perversion," said Hemingway,
Of such forced haste; the feelings fray and splay.

25

The Big Wave

To Michael Ridland

Others are leaving as I pull in tonight
Dressed for the chill, and under a dull sky
Gray surf from winter storms is lifting high
Far out from shore, then bouncing in loud and white,
But a kid in trunks straightens to his full height
By his old VW, powerful and—hell, I see
He is one-legged. Now he vigorously
Swings by on his crutches in the failing light.
When I look next he has got off alone
—Christ, to do what? Way down the beach, he's thrown
The crutches down and is hopping, his one thigh
In the boiling white, toward a wave three times as high
As he. Hesitates, though. The wave comes on
And he hops back. In the sad, bad light I start my run.

26

Running in America

Saint Kenneth Cooper, with your stethoscope
Stopwatch and clipboard, how they run for you!
Eager and obedient in every thew
Having had courses now on How to Cope
With Death, on how to eat, to screw, to ope-
n doors, breathe, spit, work zippers … they can do
The running but you make it all come true
In charts, with points, paying off Faith and Hope:
Dad in his old sweat suit, running head down
Doggedly in the dusk, the stern beauty with the frown,
The young couple goose-stepping *shoulder*-high,
Eyes straight ahead, to warm up—none of them smiles.
I've heard at parties the questions … "How many miles …?"
And the really serious runner's shy reply.

At the New School for Social Research you can take not only "Coping with Death" but "The Philosophy and Psychology of Death." "We were early in death studies," says the New School's proud president, John R. Everett.

27

Light Like the Beautiful Trout Fly Name: Pale Evening Dun

Cold spatter of rain, then wind. Last night the tide
Covering the beach and sliding up the rocks
Along the cliffs, driving the sanderling flocks
And me elsewhere, now a beach five yards wide
All kelp-heaps and scattered stones, and a rock-slide
At the point, wet shale in jagged blocks
Angled for twists, foot-slitherings, bone-shocks;
And pooled and trickling water on every side.
I rock-hop past the next point. Here the air
Is quiet, the ocean crump-crumping its tons
Well out from shore, the nearby water still ...
Stretch of smooth sand! with a boulder here and there,
Standing alone—black rock, gray water, duns
Of wet sand, cloud-roofed, in the even light; so beautiful.

28

Running in the Rain, High Tide

Rain slanting past and no place here to run.
In the cold deepening dusk there comes the roar
Of water much too near; as the car door
Caught by a gust swings wide, I see the brown
Waves smack the cliffs. Well, head for the next beach down.
Bulldozers have gouged it up and gullies pour
With the runoff, crumbling, forcing me to detour
Through garbage to the blacktop (it's near town).
I run in a dazzle of streetlights and car lights
My glasses streaming, and splattering along
Alone, think of the swaggering word invictus;
And sprint back through the drench against a strong
Headwind, wearing as the car comes into sight
A combination grin and runner's rictus.

29

Christmas Down at the Mission

Tonight sun and moon and earth line up and drag
The sea far back, the still tidepools, like light
Solidified, mirror that great headlight,
The low sun, beaming on … but here's the snag:
Been reading in the latest lit'ry rag
From Britain, and in this one doing right
(As with the Pauper Witch) is their delight
In tight-lipped "leaders." Made my spirits flag.
I know it's for your own good when they say
"Sit down, my friend, this chilling Christmas day,
Though the bench is hard, the table bare of trimmings,
Hold out your bowl and heed our bracing hymnings!"
Meat gray and stringy, gravy gray and thin,
Served up by the clammy enemies of literary sin.

30

Freezing

I pick my way through a parking lot nearly full
As a miscellaneous, chilly crowd straggles in.
The sea is pale, a barely fluttering skin
Of light, and everywhere, an uncomfortable
Clearness and separateness to things, they have all
Hardened in this sharp air, and I begin
My run bleakly, not much helped out when
A new girl jogger flashes me a smile
For my weak smile; much less when I look off
From the stones underfoot to where there glows
The sun, low now and like a blurred red rose
In its cold cloud. The cold moon clears the bluff,
Full, and almost too bright to look into.
I head home running moonlit through and through.

Running in the Early January Cold

The near water heaves bright gray, then deepening
Outward to a dark horizon line as keen
And aloof as the evenly moving, clean
Crest of a wave, or the edge of a gull's wing:
That pale sunset out there hasn't anything
To do with me, with its cloud whorl, its icy green;
There's nothing in the few people I've seen
To catch the eye, and take away the sting
Of the raw cold look of things; and thinking I run
Upright and briskly, I see my shadow: a tall
Pinhead aslant on stilts, going at a crawl
Along the sand; and in that room today
The neutral silence, I feeling in all I say
The desolateness of what's barely begun.

32

The House that Cliff-hangs

Sometimes my run down here's like putting on
Music and after a while not listening.
I tell myself I spot every least thing
As the same, or changed, around me as I run,
And now I see, as the last third of the sun
At the horizon lays a glistening
Road to the house and reddens the west wing,
That the cliff has fallen away. The deck is gone.
There's a piece of railing stopping in mid-air
Above the expanse of raw vertical clay,
Loose dirt, iceplant, and planking sprawled down here,
Storm-loosened—not today or yesterday.
Coming back by in the late dusk I see
The bearded young man contemplating me
    Or else the wreckage there,
    Through the salt atmosphere,
Straight down, from his high, narrow balcony.

33

Willets under an Overcast

This new and winter term is a stopped wheel
To push against, it budges and rolls back
Into its rut in a hard-frozen track
Through the inside country where I think and feel:
Outside the willets land for their evening meal,
Their lifted wings exposing elegant black
And white zigzags, beside the tidal slack:
Gray clouds, gray ocean, and the light still and pale.
Whatever was missing from what I did today
Is the second overcast to run under here,
I puzzle and puzzle under it all the way
To my turn-back place—willets again, a pair
Alight on a black rock offshore, crying *kerlear!*
Teetering prettily, above the sloshing gray.

34

The Nympholept

The crimson sun slipping down through the haze
Smoothly as I arrived is now half gone,
Its color riding the backwash; and I run
And sketch a plan to draw out of her daze
Of shyness Pam who writes so well, and faze
The Marxist glibnesses maybe of Juan,
When the girl walks by, barefoot, putting down
Footprints still clear under the water glaze.
Later, it's two girls writing in notebooks
As I come in, in the deep dusk they lean
To see their words. Then still another looks
My way as I get in my car, to say
"Yer a good runner!" I, startled: "Nah."—"I've seen
You often ..." drifts through the gloom as she goes her way.

35

The Bare Winter Beach

No kites, no frisbees. No baking half the day
Beside her friend, a radio in between.
No babies. Not a six-pack to be seen,
Even gulls are scarce (no garbage). Far away
Is the big brown belly July puts on display.
—Two lovers, and one walker, dark and lean,
And two runners, are strung out on the clean
Smooth beach ahead, with the light a misty gray
Coming from nowhere and everywhere alike.
A good place for a passion to be worked out
Or up. Near here last night my young friend Mike
Whose wife left him and took their child, did not
See me run by, his eyes so fixed on a pair
Of beauties running by with streaming hair
(Eyes that have been in training on Vermeer).

36

Running with Another *TLS* Poem
in my Head

The bulge of the sea above the benches shows
High tide, and I'll be driven off the sand
Onto the rocks. I should have calmly planned
My run, by the tide-chart, but old drip-nose
Reading his Homer troubled my repose,
Reading his *Times* indeed almost unmanned
Me with his questions. He can't understand
Why gods and heroes cause so many woes.
Odysseus, with his lies and murders—not a bit nice!
Couldn't he practice a gentler kind of vice?
These Afghans, skinning the Russian infidel
Alive! Blood-smeared old Faiths, awake and well,
Inflicting on us still their gruesome folly ...
Why can't we all be good, and kind, and jolly?

37

Running in the Rain Again;
a Swede with Stout Legs

I run and think of running here the night
After the first big rainstorm of the year,
And the tide low, just a few people here,
Wave-watchers, mostly, shapes making upright
Thick ink-strokes on the louring watery light
Between gray waves and low clouds, and the air
Sharp and the beach vast, gaunt (with here and there
Rank kelp-heaps), bending flatly out of sight.
I'd finished fast and started cooling out,
There's a big Swede nearby doing same,
Stretching and bending and then gazing about—
And edging my way, I see, as if by aim;
He says, "It's beautiful, in its own way,"
Walking past. "Yeh, it's beautiful," I say.

38

Running

Driving down with KABC Sports-talk on,
Author of *The Complete Runner* is the guest,
"How should you breathe?" he's asked, "What is the best
Surface for running?" "Is the backbone jarred when you run?"…
Now that the days are longer, now that the sun
Is up where it blinds me when I'm running west
And the plovers are leaving, all too soon the rest
Of the signs of winter down here will be gone.
Still, Dad in his old sweat suit and salt-caked shoes
Sends me a wave this time, abrupt and shy,
Without turning his head, and others smile
As *they* pass, and now my mind cuts out, while
In that sudden sort of silence that ensues
When an engine stops, the cliffs blur by.…

39

Big Waves in Wind and Clear Cold Sunlight, and the Intelligent New Secretary from the Main Office

Clear from the entrance I could see the spray
Glistening above the cartops like the snow
That banners off the drifts in a big blow,
And once I'm running I watch the falling away
Of waves heaved house-high, and the steady play
Of the cold light on wave-slopes bursting snow
Over the snowy rush and crush below—
Too much for surfers: wave-watchers here today.
And up the beach, a girl sitting quietly
On a big rock, with those waves roaring in.
And it is Marilyn, I recognize
As I come near; sun lights her gold hairpin,
And I start wondering if her blue eyes
Are seeing more than the rest of us down here see.

40

Old Rocks out in the Late Light

Chill air and the sea sunk, like a lake
In drought-time, back from the gray sand,
A bright place the size of a man's hand
On the waves, where the light comes through a break
In low clouds. And the striped rocks. They take
The eye between flat sea and land,
Humped, leaning, pale band by dark band,
Green-bearded, dripping, with pools that quake
In the raw breeze. Here's one pokes out
At our cliffs a heavy upper jaw
That with the lower grips in its maw
The sand I cross. Surely the brief light
Is holy, and holy the darkness light
Makes when it goes, but not that snout.

41

A Quiet Fourth

83

Homesick, building a fly rod on the patio
All the fresh sunny breezy morning; a calm blue
Sky and green leaves close me in. Low tide's at two,
And I'll run then. —The dusty parade and rodeo
Took place in town, all right, forty-five years ago,
A thousand miles away; fireworks afterwards, too,
And then the ride home on the dirt road, winding through
The cool fields in darkness, hearing the water flow
Over the weirs; and then our dogs, at the driveway turn.
—And winter's the time for Hendry's Beach; therefore I'll write
This one, to do for my few summer runs down here:
Beach flat, trampled, sea flat, slack and warm and clear;
People little black figures against the big silver light;
Close up, it's beer can, frisbee, radio, sunburn.

—July 4, 1978

42

A Quiet Fourth

Fran and I much alone this bright mild day
With the boys scattered, friends too, mostly, so
It's Sousa and Ives out on the patio
(And how subtly the Ives lets the attention stray);
Then work on a fly rod, later get away
For a run at Hendry's, when the tide is low.
My last run down there was six weeks ago—
Summer crowds, and a new fee I won't pay.
But on the Fourth you want a crowd, I learn,
So down I go: beach flat, sea calm, clear, warm.
In and beside it, in every tint, size, form,
People, with frisbee, radio, sunburn.
—Drive back, see centered formally on a top stair
A beer, beneath a flag limp in the cooling air.

—July 4, 1978

43

The Other Runner

Recalling, during a drought, a rainy day last year

Wind spread the rain across the glass, I hearing it
While reading Milton all day long, and looking up
From time to time, to wonder when it would stop,
And then forgetting rain, in the warm room where I sat.
Then arriving at the beach: yellow-brown breakers lit
From under a slowly lifting ledge of cloud—the tops
Catching the level blaze, and darkness soon to drop,
And for my run the sand wave-beaten hard and flat.
I ran alone, leaving some saunterers behind,
Beside a set of fresh footprints so far apart
I couldn't match them long, and slowed my pace, resigned;
Thinking of Milton, no, of every excellence
How it exhilarates and humiliates the heart;
High waves nearing both sets of our footprints.

44

Dog-days I
Rain-running Recalled

Hard wind, rain; I the only one out here.
Wind on my back, rattle of rain on hat,
Hissing of rain on sand, and beyond that
The noise of the big waves; and small and clear
A whimbrel's call in the din as I draw near
A roaring down the cliff and over the flat
Hard beach—an hour-old river I halt at,
My glasses streaming. The world is a bright smear.
Into a gale now, and the ocean sound
Drowned out by the new howling of the air
Around my head, then even louder pounds
The *hough! hough!* of my lungs inside this blur
Of boisterous air, cliffs, water—startled mind
Along for the ride, body with its old kind.

—August 11, 1978

45
Dog-days II
Incidentally Recalling a Dying Seal

—Not that its old kind give a damn for it.
For us who live here, the impersonal
Bright quiet gaze of that dying animal
Put rightly the relation of the fit
And unfit both, to that of which we're knit.
And once the indifference is mutual
Shall consciousness here in the individual
Turn with the whole? the light of light be lit?
I know I saw that seal dying his death
Half sunk into the sand, on the sunny shore
In the tide-wash: with each wave coming in,
The sand sucking him deeper than before,
The water swirling over his head again,
Subsiding, he catching another breath.

46

Anniversary

Life's uneventful, and while we were gone
The season turned; the winter birds are here
And the crowds gone, and the salt atmosphere
Is sharper, with a low hazed-over sun
Laying its wide and glittery roadway on
Gray ocean that looks lonely. Like last year.
—Over the cliffs two hang-gliders appear,
Slope in and land nearby; I start my run.
Sand smooth, smooth! for a runner or a flyer
In this gray light and chill air's misty blend
And the sanderlings, lively, lovely, never tire,
And the sun suddenly lights a deep red fire
Up on the sand, using a beer can end,
And all of it makes up my heart's desire.

47

The Partly-written Page

Life's uneventful. What I remember most
At the odd moment or lying awake
At three A.M. is not the storms that shake
Oranges from the groves on up the coast
And wash them out to sea (this year some crossed
The bows of fishermen watching gray whales break),
Litter the shore with splintered trees and make
The news: X houses ruined, X lives lost.
What has stayed with me is such a thing as this:
I come in through the late dusk from my run,
A girl at the picnic table glances over
A half a page of writing she's just done,
Then stares out where the dark waves slap and hiss
Under the darker rainy low cloud-cover.

48

Company

There's Giles again, the lanky fellow who,
Working toward a Ph.D. in Greek,
Likes girls (and always runs with one, a sleek
Beauty at that, mirabile dictu).
—But there's one running because she was told to
By *Runner's World*. And some journalist has the cheek
To call on us to go, seek out the weak
And sick and scorned: we happy running few …
Loneliness is not possible for this
Long distance runner; I spend my mother wit
Dodging the latest book you dare not miss,
This goddamned merchandiser plucks my sleeve,
Holistic priests approach—I bob and weave,
I detour past the bull- and the horseshit.

49

The *Rebecca Mae*

97

After the loud storm she lay off shore low
In the water, grating on rocks. Then a huge wave
Beached her and she looked good enough to save,
Engine and all. Half sunk in sand now, though.
All of us eye her as we come and go,
Runners and saunterers. But she never gave
When kids tried prying her from her half grave.
Soon her name's under. Just her gunnels show.
Still the big seas aren't done with her. One day
We find her resurrected, all the way
Past the next point, then later scattered out
Against the cliff, till her last splinter's under
The sand we pad on; now a well-buried boat
To muse on running through the water-thunder.

50

Night-piece

Lying in the long dark, insomniac,
I see it clearly: sea and beach and air
And a red winter sun, down low, for fire,
For the fourth element made out by the Greek
On Sicily's coast two dozen centuries back—
Fire that'll turn me into atmosphere
After I'm dead, and ashes tossed out where
Maybe they'll wash ashore. I hear gulls creak,
And put my being in with the elements
We share with the whole show, rather than
With the odd creature in it that is man
Or with my self, still odder … till the tense
Weavings of wakefulness begin to fray
Loosen and come apart and float away—

Phrasing in lines 11 and 12 taken from Santayana's *Dialogues in Limbo.*

continued

Not bad, for night thoughts, but as Hemingway
Noticed, night thoughts on recollection,
Deep as you went for them, don't pass inspection
Laid out and drying in the light of day.
Something on which there is not much to say,
Sheer Nothingness, once more escapes detection,
Though disciplined minds can reach by indirection
What the imagination hides away …
Yes, *darkness, sundown, water*—take your pick
Of pictures: wings, a little boat, dark blue
Of gentians, you can't make any of it stick.
So human, moving, lovely, and untrue.
By the fresh light of morning being bound
To thought that makes the phrase, if not resounding, sound.

51

Sanderlings Here

A low fog bank to run inside today,
Wave-noises muffled, near cliffs blurred and pale.
Fog-puffs come down, each spreading a black tail,
A black bill aimed at the sand. And a slight gray
Movement ahead suddenly swerves this way
And a whole flock gleams cleanly purposeful
Against the drifting vapor. Now they all
Vanish up there, sheering themselves away.
And near the finish, a flat stretch, bits of shells
And pebbles lift a little and begin
To travel along the water ahead of me—
Sanderlings, running in the fog or else
Low-gliding, I here running heavily
As faintly they shape unshape and shape again.

52

"Who prop, thou ask'st,
in these bad days, my mind?"

Yeh, summer beach, young riders thudding past
Punching out clear hoofprints beside the white
Spill of the waves, against the low sun's light
The black shapes of the horsemen dwindling fast,
And here, attached to each of the sand-crumbs cast
Beside the hoofprints, a little stalactite
Of shadow, while I mope along and fight
The gloom my reading's put me in last …
Cheer up. What if you must throw in your lot
With Gittingses and Thompsons now, and not
Go back to those they've told on for the ages,
Those monsters Hardy and Frost. You'll get, God knows,
A generous friend in Lawrance Thompson's pages,
Largeness of soul in Robert Gittings' prose.

Gittings records with approval the verdict of Mr. Clodd that in Hardy "There was
no largeness of soul."

53

Running with the Pollution

I run and coordinating agencies
A panel of experts new measures called for
The decision-making process funding more
Multi-disciplinary activities
Are in my fatty tissues and all these
Are in my liver supervision war
On crime fact-finding panel a hard core
The underlying causes facilities:
Well, that's our social climate and the air
Carries their fumes and particles everywhere
We breathe. But here's one runner that keeps clear
Of *etic structures* and such—I hear the first
Fibers of these, if you come in or near,
Will cause the alveoli in your lungs to burst.

54

Slinking Off

Open the morning paper, what do you see?
Tom L. and Abby W. in full stride,
The splendid young pair running side by side,
Their dog loping between them happily
The finishing touch: I wish them well all three
And damn the lurking journalist who eyed
And caught them coming toward him in their pride
And put them there, a soon-yellowing cliché.
Picture one now, with his thin legs, gray hair
And turkey neck and flapping khaki pants
And nylon shell from the discount drug store
Slipping along down here and wondering
If some other poet ... deepening in advance
His shame at doing *so* fashionable a thing.

55

Pelican Halcyon

Low tide of winter, beach shines to the eye
Wide as the sea itself for my late run
And the sea light-streaked and smoothed out to a sun
Red in horizon fog, and already high
A piece of the moon's rim, in the neuter sky.
Quiet. Sun flattens to an oval on
The fogbank; to a glowing bar; then gone.
And in the pallor, one pelican flaps by,
Black on the afterglow; and another, black
Out on the pale sea, silently splashing down
Makes yet another pelican silhouette
With the thrown water; I seeing this all alone,
It happens, with the one sound as I head back
The slip-slap of my feet along the wet.

56

Spell Breaking

That is soon over, others come in view:
Old man in street clothes down for a beach walk,
Three women heading back absorbed in talk,
A guy surf-fishing, the odd runner or two.
And no more pelicans: gulls now skreak and mew,
I scare a willet that flies to a safe rock
Kerlear-ing his hurt feelings, a godwit flock
Reflects in the shine they poke their long bills through.
And here's my old friend Herb, facing the sea,
Musing, quite motionless, holding, curiously,
A folded newspaper level with his waist:
Day-offering to sea and sundown, he the priest.
I can't not greet him though the spell will break,
He jogs on in with me for old and new times' sake.

57

Coming Down to Run in Dark and Fog

In the near dark two runners stagger in
Out of the coiling fog along the shore.
Another lurches in, and then two more.
But nobody else here after I begin.
Once I am startled, when the fog-swirls thin,
By a movement I glimpse behind me on the shore.
That's the moon's hard reflection. Airliner's roar
Joins wave-roar for one huge roar coming in
Straight after me; and then a hooded form
Comes by with darkness where the face should show;
It's a runner, though. Small light, with sea below
Is the cliff-house, fog-faint, the one a storm
Last year brought down in part, to crash and splinter,
What's left now pushing into one more winter.

58

Heron Out There

The first cold day of winter, darkness near,
A stiff wind coming in and a high tide
Roaring inshore and everyone else inside
Or heading there, what am I doing here
Plugging through mushy sand, with a wind tear
In either eye, up a beach three feet wide ...
Chased by a rush of water up the side
Of the shale at the first point, I slog from there
To the furthest—and the heron I know by day
Is a slab of the dark rock, breaking away
To pass me in the dusk. Down beach again
I spot his still shape—leaf with a long stem.
When I come near he flaps unhurriedly,
Belongingly, into the icy spray,
    Then back the other way
    From me, this time to stay
The long night undisturbed, by the loud sea.

59

The Honesty Boys

I run along beside the little wobbly blur
Of the moon on the sleek wet sand (whereas in the sky
It's holding motionless, hatchet-sharp) and have an eye
On the just-after-sundown ocean's crinkling stir
In the beautiful steel-blue light that suddenly appears,
And find myself thinking again about the way
Certain poets are always putting on a display
Of *honesty*—they bring up yours, and of course theirs,
To your face; sometimes slyly, showing how others are
Dishonest—as one of them just lately tried to tell
All of us Hardy was. That didn't turn out well.
However, credit for trying.... On with the essay-war
With each name mentioned being a piece of disputed terrain,
Or outpost in the latest *honesty* campaign.

The Desolation Light

I came down here one dusk and the beach was gone.
The winter tides were easing it out to sea,
Shelving it down and down, when suddenly
A storm came through and scoured it to the stone—
A jumble of stone; and the sky having done
Its damage loosened up, pale vacancy
Between a lot of ragged cloud debris
Scattering fast, foam yellow and waves brown,
The sea, too, loosened and sprawling, sunk so low
That stubs of rock under for months now showed.
Air darkened as if a curtain had been drawn,
And shining as if for meditating on
Was a tidepool that the gray light had filled
To brimming where a simple stillness held.

61

News

RAVAGED BY NATURE, says the local News,
BEACHES ARE DYING—naturally I read on,
How one day these thin margins will be gone
For good, new sand held back by the dams we use
On our best streams while the sea slowly chews
The old away, back to the cliffs and down
To the stones. And nowhere then to run or sun.
Any dark place can say what else you'll lose:
The canyon air that floats the alder leaf,
The light on the creek, and the creek too, will go;
And the ground under, where it had to flow.
Your sons, and the dear woman who is half your life,
And the two eyes you see both with and through
Will go; and your skeleton; and your spirit, too.

62

Heron Shapes at Dusk

I know the heron that's made this beach his own
Between the headlands, slants like a poised spear
Invisible in the driftwood where I peer—
And there he goes now, flapping off alone.
Later his shape breaks out of some gray stone
That the low tides leave bare this time of year,
Then further down, in deeper dusk, lifts clear
Where only a black tangle of kelp had shown.
Then over by the cliffs, in the near dark there,
I see a heron shape become a girl
Hunched with her trouble there on the driftwood.
The shore a place of human bad and good,
Not herons now, so stony stark her stare
At the late red fading from a cloud-swirl.

63

Noon Swimmers, Plovers,
a Young Heron, a Grebe

People are black on silver this mid-day
Far up the beach, the waves withdrawing show
Light rustling in the grit, the plovers throw
Shadows appearing solider than they,
And the young heron that lives here flaps away
And alights up ahead in the backflow
That glares more silver as it slips below
The nubs of the bright foam, the sunny spray,
While the grebe I come on has been lying dead,
At the water's edge, on his back. His wings are spread
As if in flight. He looks heraldic, too—
Like the scrawny phoenix D.H. Lawrence drew.
But this bird's missing an eye; draggled and sad
Lies here for a little the only self he had.

64

Heron Totem

Up the long beach, a flock of sanderlings
Will swoop past a ridge of ocean roaring near
(Their white chests flashing), tilt and disappear,
Or pelicans line up, dark, heavy things,
And form one body with a dozen wings
Approaching me head-on, or godwits flare
Warm cinnamon wing-linings on the gray air
When they veer off in the big flocks winter brings.
I love them all, and most this homely one:
Color of driftwood, among the bustlers, the wary
Swervers, he leans inquiringly, and waits.
Slow, frail, ungainly, set for the long run,
Silent with hope, by nature solitary,
He picks his spot, stands still, and concentrates.

65

Politics: Reading the Papers

On the first page, review of Brecht by Spender.
Asks the tough question last: how come he
Clammed up about Stalin?—Because, you see,
Brecht could "play games with evil," with no tender
Conscience, for the sake of future good. (I render
The prose down to its shred of meat.) Page three,
It's Solzhenitsyn—getting by memory
His prose and verse, in the gulag. Old non-bender.
And in the *News*, Bukovsky (Vladimir,
I mean): "I don't like certain ideas because
They bring terrible results." *His* prose is clear.
"The most dangerous thing is when you start
To limit your conscience" *for the noble cause....*
Cold dusk, and time to run ... where's the tide-chart?

66

Sunday Run: Starting Out

At the water's edge a baby smacks the beach,
Seriously, then casts me a grave look.
A woman wades along reading a book,
Surf tugging at her legs. And the gulls screech,
And a girl makes a staggering run and reach
For a frisbee through a haze of charcoal smoke
Sharp-scented in the cool air, from a nook
Under the cliffs. We brown and burn and bleach.
And the sober sun, half through the afternoon,
Throws iris-leaf shapes, and squarish glares of light
Along the rollers, sends a quick-sliding thread
Of light along a crest, and overhead
Makes on a softball on its climbing flight
In the blue, a tiny daytime quarter moon.

67

In Public: *Liberté, Fraternité*

A photographer sets his tripod up and waits
Among various types down here for the sunset;
The unlovely public—whatever it is creates
Us bungles us…. And no colors as yet;
The scuffed-up sand shines gray where it is wet.
The place seems idly jostled, by the gazes
And glances of all these folk, their grunts and phrases.
On the bright gray they bulk in silhouette.

~

And home now, out of the salt atmosphere,
With these things written as I pleased I feel
The doubts crowd in (like a real crowd, watching me
Running along down there), each all too real
And undisguisable deformity
Passing in plain view, in the open here.

68

What the Sea Muttered

with a variation on a theme of Goya

You haven't kept the reader busy enough.
I know, I know—it comes of my long affair
With the clear and ordinary; all my care
May fail to hold the intensity in the stuff.
Too many off-rhymes, rhythms strained and rough,
You crash the delicate old barrier
Between octave and sestet. I declare
My shame before the masters. *You sheer off*
From the whole truth: not even writing of
That day you found you'd fallen out of love
With running down here, much less of harder themes.
—The reason sleeps, and monsters shape the dreams
Which are the things we're doing in broad day,
The monstrous half-done.... Nolo contendere.

69

What the Wind Hissed

A chill gray day and a wind began to blow:
Where will you get with that plain water style?
Running's a joke that long since has gone stale,
Seascapes were old a century ago.
I like plain words, I always have been slow.
And the names you drop. Milton of course is vile,
And Hemingway! pathetic macho male …
And that brute, Robert Frost. I like them, though.
Why Santayana? Surely you want Saussure.
And Rilke's missing. Really I much prefer
Hardy. *He's fading fast.* Herbert? *OK …*
And Homer? *Fine.* My dirty words? *Passé.*
Here, try a Barthes. Somehow it lacks allure,
Such is my hesychastic mood today.

70

Topophilia

Cold dead light, and the beach, from the long rain,
Like a mud-flat under this low cloud-cope; though where
Sun lights the cloud's far edge a pane of clear
Yellow sky joins it to the steady line
Of the horizon; and tiny and black, and fine
In detail, an oil rig sits precisely there
On the skyline, like some miniature
Electronic component, the thin struts showing plain.
And the space out there clear and empty and fine,
Ready for God to fill—like an Inness, a Lane,
Or even a Hopper: and I think of their
Frank and mystical love of light, and plain
Shapes in the great vacancies of air,
And taking comfort in the bare and spare.

Hopper, to whom the 'mystical' doesn't exactly apply, said, 'What I wanted to do was to paint the sunlight on the side of a house.' Inness spoke of 'the hidden story of the real.' With Lane I had especially in mind the wonderful *Owl's Head, Maine.*—Santayana writes of the 'something in the human spirit (which is not merely human), something unreclaimed and akin to the elements,' that is perhaps at work in these things.

Running at Sundown and Dark

Well, it's a pretty sunset—sherbet green,
Orange, even some raspberry, streak the sky
From sea horizon to cliffs. Pelicans ply
The offshore reaches and fishing boats careen
On big waves, giving substance to the scene
With their everyday skillful efforts. Meanwhile I,
Pondering a talk that may well go awry,
Run on the tide-zone's particolored sheen:
Mind pawing obsessively at certain unclear
Distinctions.... Pass two more runners; lovers, one pair;
A lone girl walking slowly back. It's night
When I come in, distinctions still not right,
Past black stumps in the water just off shore—
Surfers, in the dark there, waiting for one more.

About the Author

Alan Stephens was born December 19, 1925, in Greeley, Colorado. He grew up on the family farm there, and served in the U.S. Army Air Corps. Thanks to the G.I. Bill, he attended Colorado State Teacher's College (now the University of Northern Colorado), the University of Colorado at Boulder, the University of Denver, and the University of Missouri. He received bachelor's and master's degrees from DU, and a Ph.D. from Missouri.

Stephens taught English at Arizona State University from 1954 to 1960, with a year at Stanford on a fellowship (1956–1957). He joined the faculty at the University of California, Santa Barbara, in 1960 and remained there until his retirement in 1989, except for a year at DU (1967–1968). He was a founding faculty member of the College of Creative Studies at UCSB.

He was married for 60 years to Frances Stephens. They raised three sons. He died July 21, 2009, at home in Santa Barbara. He may be found in his verses.

This sonnet sequence was originally published as a part of *In Plain Air* (1982). Here, lines 13 and 14 of sonnet 43, and line 14 of sonnet "50 continued," are taken from early manuscript versions. There are a few other minor revisions, mostly in punctuation.

A.A.S.

www.ingramcontent.com/pod-product-compliance
Lightning Source LLC
Chambersburg PA
CBHW031334060726
47590CB00007B/2458